Table Of Contents

Introduction

> You can make many plans, but the LORD's purpose will
> prevail.
>
> Proverbs 19:21 (NLT)

We live in a day and time that many on this earth have lost purpose
and direction; where many are seeking wisdom and counsel for the
answers to their problems and circumstances. This is a day and time
that the securities of life are being shaken to a point of desperation
and confusion.

In the Midst of all this God has given us the answers, He has given
us a GPS system that can not break or misguide us. Many are man's
purposes and plans but at the end of the day only God's Purposes
will Prevail. If you are a Christian, God has given you the answer –
its not far away locked in a cave somewhere –

God has given us answers and direction in this life as well as in the
time to come. God's Holy Word – the Bible has the answer for
mankind in these perilous times. Not only has God given us His
Word but He has given His people His Holy Spirit to lead us and
guide us in the right direction.

In this book you will discover the Truths and Blessings of Living the
New Life in God's Prevailing Purpose. As New Creations in Christ –
as New Covenant Christians living in the New Covenant of Grace
we have the advantage of succeeding in the purpose of God on this
earth.

> For we are God's [*own*] handiwork (His workmanship),
> recreated in Christ Jesus, [*born anew*] that we may do those
> good works which God predestined (planned beforehand) for
> us [*taking paths which He prepared ahead of time*], that we
> should walk in them [*living the good life which He
> prearranged and made ready for us to live*].
>
> Ephesians 2:10 (Amp.)

For we are God's masterpiece. He has created us anew in Christ Jesus, so we can do the good things He planned for us long ago.

Ephesians 2:10 (NLT)

Chapter 1

A New Creation

> Therefore if any man be in Christ, he is a new creature: old
> things are passed away; behold, all things are become new.
> 2 Corinthians 5:17

The foundation for every believer should start with this scripture. I
will use this scripture many times in this book. Repetition is needed
in order to really catch the heart of God. Do not just skim over this
scripture but read it slowly and stop and think, meditate and even
speak it out of your mouth.

To be a New Creation means to be a New Species that never existed
before. A Brand New Person with a Brand New Heart with a Brand
New Start. Today can be your New Day to Live your New Life with
God's Prevailing Purpose. When a person accepts Jesus Christ and
gives their heart and life to Him, in turn He gives them His Heart
and Life.

Christianity is not a religion, it's a relationship with God and a
Supernatural Life, It's a Life that we receive. Eternal Life is not a
place in heaven, but the actual Heart and Life of God given to you in
place of your heart and life. Eternal Life is something that we can
experience here on earth, it is part of being a New Creation.

The First Man and Woman: From Life to Death

Divine, Eternal life was the kind of life God intended for man to
enjoy on this earth. But when Adam and Eve sinned, an immediate
separation between God and man took place.

God had told Adam and Eve that two trees stood in the Garden: the
tree of life and the tree of the knowledge of good and evil. God
commanded them not to eat of the tree of the knowledge of good and
evil, warning them,

"...In the day that you eat of it you shall surely die" (Gen. 2:17).

Adam and Eve ate of the forbidden fruit. God's words were very clear. He said, "...*In the day that you eat of it you shall surely die.*" Adam and Eve died spiritually at the moment of their disobedience, although they remained physically alive. At the very moment they ate of that fruit, they went through a major change—literally being taken out of life and into death.

Multitudes of people are walking on this earth today who remain dead, even though their bodies are still alive. They are dead souls walking, until a person connects with God and makes Jesus the Lord of his life - until God's Eternal Life and Resurrection power lives on the inside of him—that person is just a walking dead man.

The story of the gospel is the story of God's commitment to mankind to provide a way for man to escape the destiny of eternal death and a physical hell and to once more be able to experience His divine, Eternal Life. Jesus went all the way into death and hell so He can make available the Free Gift of Eternal Life to every man and woman on the face of the earth!

Regeneration *"Ye Must be born again"*

"All praise to God, the Father of our Lord Jesus Christ. It is by His great mercy that we have been born again, because God raised Jesus Christ from the dead. Now we live with great expectation, " 1 Peter 1:3 NLT

We are New creations in Christ Jesus, we are born again, born from above, our spirits, our hearts have been changed, and now the Holy Spirit lives inside us. We don't desire to sin anymore like we used to. This change on the inside of us is described in scripture by different terms here are just a few for now.

1. "Born a New" - Eph. 2:10 (Amp.)

2. "Creating anew" – Eph. 4:24

3. "Begetting" James 1:18

4. "Born of God" – 1 John 5:1, 4-5

5. "Quickening" – John 5:21; Eph. 2:5

6. "Called out of darkness into marvelous light" – 1 Peter 2:9

7. "Regenerated" or "Regeneration" – Titus 3:5

Those who have experienced this New Birth have become Born A - New. The scriptures further describe the people who have received this New Life as:

1. To be "Alive from the dead" or "made alive" – Rom. 6:13; Eph. 2:1

2. To be "God's workmanship" – Eph. 2:10

3. To be "New Creations" – Gal. 6:15; 2 Corin. 5:17

4. To be "born again" or "born from above" – John 3:3,7; 1 Peter 1:23

5. To be " born of the Spirit" John 3:6, 8

The scriptures make it clear that we must have this experience. Some people think that eternal life is the life they will have when they get to Heaven. Eternal life, however, is something we have right now! Eternal life is the life of God. It is the God-kind of life. Eternal life is the nature of God, which comes into our spirit to recreate us and make us a new creature; to change our nature. If you have Accepted Christ, you have within you the nature of God, which is love;

"By this shall all men know that ye are my disciples, if ye have love one to another" John 13:35

When we have been born again and have the nature of God abiding within us, we can develop our spirit to higher levels. It is very important that after we are Born – A- New that we find a good Bible Teaching and Preaching Church where you can get the Word of God. Thank God church is not the only place where you can get the Word of God, in these days and times we have the Bible taught on T.V., radio, internet and books, cd's and Dvd's.

It is very important that you get planted in a church under a Good Anointed Pastor who can care for you spiritually and feed you the Word of God. Someone you can talk to and ask questions in order to learn as you continue to read your Bible and feed on the Word of God.

"Whereby are given unto us exceeding great and precious promises: that by these ye might be partakers of the divine nature, having escaped the corruption that is in the world through lust" 2 Peter 1:4

When you became a child of God, God imparted His own nature - eternal life - to you. This life, this nature, this being, instantly changed your spirit. You passed from spiritual death, into life.

"If we love our Christian brothers and sisters, it proves that we have passed from death to life. But a person who has no love is still dead" 1 John 3:14 NLT

You passed from the dominion of Satan into the dominion of Christ. When you received eternal life, the sinful, selfish nature was taken out of you. The corruption from which you have escaped is spiritual death, the sinful nature

"And because of His glory and excellence, He has given us great and precious promises. These are the promises that enable you to share His divine nature and escape the world's corruption caused by human desires" 2 Peter 1:4 NLT

That sinful nature was actually taken out of you. Second Corinthians 5:17 states, "...old things are passed away...." And God's nature came into you. Now you are a partaker of God's divine nature - the nature of God - the life of God! If you have been born again, God's life is in you, God's nature is in you, God's ability is in you, God's wisdom is in you. You are partakers of His divine nature and character now.

Chapter 2

A New Life

"For as the Father hath life in himself; so hath he given to the Son to have life in himself" John 5:26

The original manuscripts of the Bible are written in three main languages, Hebrew (Old Testament), Greek (New Testament) as well as in Aramaic. In order to get the true meaning of the Bible sometimes we must look at the original languages. The Greek word translated "life" is zoe. It is pronounced zo-aye. There are three other Greek words in the New Testament are translated as "*life.*" These words and their meanings are: "*psuche,*" which means natural life, or human life; "*bios,*" which means manner of life; and "*anastrophe,*" which means behavior.

Zoe means eternal life, God's life or The God Kind of Life. It is God's nature. It is life as God has it - that which the Father has in Himself - and that which the Incarnate Son has in Himself. In the New Testament it is called eternal life, everlasting life, and sometimes just life.

It doesn't matter what "manner of life" or "behavior" you have right now, it will not do you any good unless you have zoe! And that's what Jesus came to bring you! Jesus said in John 10:10 "*I Am come that you may have Life and have it more Abundantly*"

For as the Father has this Zoe - Life in Himself, so He has given to the Son to have Zoe - Life in Himself. We are made New Creations in Christ and that new creature lives in the image of Jesus Christ, Who is the express image of the Father! Your spirit man has been resurrected with the same new life with which He made Jesus alive.

But God! So rich is He in His mercy! Because of and in order to satisfy the great and wonderful and intense love with which He loved us, Even when we were dead [slain] by [our own] shortcomings and trespasses, He made us alive together in fellowship and in union with Christ. He gave us the very life of Christ Himself, the same new life with which He quickened Him.... **Ephesians 2:4-5 AMP**

Colossians tells us that we have the potential to become fully spiritually mature:

For in Him the whole fullness of Deity (the Godhead), continues to dwell in bodily form—giving complete expression of the divine nature. And you are in Him, made full and have come to fullness of life—in Christ you too are filled with the Godhead: Father, Son and Holy Spirit, and reach full spiritual stature. And He is the Head of all rule and authority—of every angelic principality and power. **Colossians 2:9-10 AMP**

God has given us Himself, His very own nature, His own substance, His life. We call it eternal life. The Bible also calls it *resurrection life*. You actually have the same new life God gave Jesus when He raised Him from the dead residing on the inside of you.

So how do we get that resurrection life to affect our daily walk with the Lord and to affect our circumstances? We are to die to sin and alive to God in union with Him (Rom. 6:11).

If then you have been raised with Christ [to a new life, thus sharing His resurrection from the dead], aim at and seek the [rich, eternal treasures] that are above, where Christ is, seated at the right hand of God. **Colossians 3:1 AMP**

We must change our focus. If we keep our attention on natural things, then the power of our new life in Christ will not be manifested in us. We will remain immature Christians. We find how we are to walk in the power of this new life in Romans 7:

When we were living in the flesh (mere physical lives) the sinful passions that were awakened and aroused up by [what] the Law [makes sin] were constantly operating in our natural

powers...so that we bore fruit for death. But now we are discharged from the Law and have terminated all intercourse with it, having died to what once restrained and held us captive. So now we serve not under [obedience to] the old code of written regulations, but [under obedience to the promptings] of the Spirit in newness [of life].
Romans. 7:5-6 AMP

If you have given your life to Christ you are now a New Person with a Brand New Life on the inside of you. It is now your discipline to obey the New Life and Conscience within you. Your flesh will war against your New Life but you must discipline yourself to follow the leading of your Brand New, Born A New spirit.

"Being born again, not of corruptible seed, but of incorruptible, by the word of God, which liveth and abideth for ever" 1 Peter. 1:23

We are begotten of God. We are born of God. We are children of God. We are heirs of God. We are joint-heirs (the word "joint" means equal) with Jesus (Rom. 8:17). In declaring this, we do not magnify ourselves. We magnify God and what He has done for us through the Lord Jesus Christ. We do not make ourselves new creatures. God made us new creatures. He is the Author and Finisher of our faith. We are new creatures created by God in Christ Jesus! We are born of incorruptible seed by the living Word of God

"Then spake Jesus again unto them, saying, I am the light of the world: he that followeth me shall not walk in darkness, but shall have the light of life". John 8:12

People can have eternal life, but if they don't walk in the light of it, and take advantage of that life and nature - things won't turn out right in their lives. We as Christians have eternal life, but we have to appropriate it. We have to walk in the light of it. God's life is in us. We must walk in the light of it and watch it change our life.

The Process

When the Word of God is preached to someone who has never heard the Gospel and conviction comes upon him, it's not a physical or mental feeling - he may not even understand it - but it's down deep on the inside. The Spirit of God through the Word of God is contacting the spirit of that person and convicting him of sin.

When that man responds to the call of God and the Gospel message, his spirit is born again. His spirit is recreated by receiving eternal life. Receiving eternal life is the most miraculous event in life. It's called the New Birth. It's called the new creation. It is God imparting His very nature to our heart and spirit.

It is described in 2 Corinthians 5:17 and 18. The New Birth is God actually giving spiritual birth to a man. And this instantaneous New Birth takes place, not in the body, not in the soul, but in the heart and spirit of man!

The spirit of man becomes a brand-new by a Miracle. This Miracle is called the New Creation in Christ. God gave us the gift of eternal life. He imparted to our spirit His very nature and character.

> "Therefore if any man be in Christ, he is a new creature: old things are passed away; behold, all things are become new" 2 Corinthians. 5:17

The moment you accept Jesus Christ as your Savior and confess Him as your Lord (Rom. 10:9-10), you, too, will be recreated, Born A-New. At that moment, the redemption which Jesus provided two thousand years ago became a reality to you. At that instant, the very life and nature of God was imparted to your spirit. You were recreated - born again!

The New Birth is an experience. It is not a religion. It is not joining a church. It is the re-birth of your spirit. When you were born again, old things passed away. In the sight of God, all sin and all of your past life was blotted out. All you had been - spiritually speaking - was blotted out, removed. You became a new man in Christ Jesus. God sees no past sins in your life, you are *Just-as-if-you'd-never-sinned.*

All things inside you became new. Your spirit was recreated. You passed from death unto life (1 John 3:14)! When you are a new creature in Christ, you are recreated. The life and nature of God come in you. You pass from death unto life!

Chapter 3

A New Heart

When we give our lives to Christ, we receive His Life, but as we give our hearts to Him, in exchange He gives us His Heart. Before we were born again, we had a sin nature and we were dead in our heart and spirit. We did not know the God Kind of Love or the God kind of Life. Those who have not received Christ are as the Bible describes in Eph. 2:1-3, dead men walking, controlled by the spirit of the world.

Sin blinds the heart and mind, and once a person completely turns, and gives their heart and life to Christ they begin to come alive in spirit with a New Life, vision and purpose. Once someone comes to Christ and receives His New Heart they also receive His Nature and Spirit. They receive a New passion for life.

In the "new birth" we get a New Heart, for a New Start.

> For I will take you from among the heathen, and gather you out of all countries, and will bring you into your own land. Then will I sprinkle clean water upon you, and ye shall be clean: from all your filthiness, and from all your idols, will I cleanse you. *A new heart* also will I give you, *and a new spirit* will I put within you: and I will take away the stony heart out of your flesh, and I will give you an heart of flesh. And I will put *my spirit within you*, and *cause you to walk in my statutes, and ye shall keep my judgments, and do [them].* And ye shall dwell in the land that I gave to your fathers; and ye shall be my people, and I will be your God. (Ezekiel 36:24-28)

In the book of Jeremiah it describes this New Heart and what it contains.

> Behold, the days come, saith the LORD, that I will make a **new covenant** with the house of Israel, and with the house of Judah: Not according to the covenant that I made with their fathers in the day *[that]* I took them by the hand to bring them out of the

land of Egypt; which my covenant they brake, although I was an husband unto them, saith the LORD: But this *[shall be]* the covenant that I will make with the house of Israel; After those days, saith the LORD, I will put ***my law in their inward parts***, and ***write it in their hearts;*** and will be their God, and they shall be my people. And they shall teach no more every man his neighbour, and every man his brother, saying, Know the LORD: for *they* shall all know me, from the least of them unto the greatest of them, saith the LORD: for I will forgive their iniquity, and I will remember their sin no more. (Jer. 31:31-34)

When we are Born again we receive: a new nature

When we receive this Divine Exchange and receive our New Heart we also receive The Love of God (Rom. 5:5; 1 Cor. 13:1-13). We receive God's desires to obey the Law of God. Both Jeremiah and Ezekiel were prophesying of the New Covenant and the Born Again Experience. In the New Covenant we have the Law of Love, and that Law is written on our new hearts as well as that Power of Love to fulfill the Law of Love fills our heart.

When we received our New Heart we also received Faith and hope (Rom. 12:3 1 Cor. 13:13). We also received all the fruit of the Spirit (Gal. 5:22-23).We will discuss later each of these but for now know that you have the character of Jesus in you through the fruit of the spirit: love, joy, peace, longsuffering, gentleness, goodness, faith, meekness, temperance.

> "As newborn babes, desire the sincere milk of the word, that ye may grow thereby" 1 Peter 2:2

When a sinner comes to Jesus, his sins are remitted - blotted out, removed. Not only are his sins blotted out and removed, but all that he was, his sinful spirit and heart are exchanged for God's Spirit and heart. His sins cease to exist. He becomes a new man in Christ Jesus. God does not see anything in that person's life before the moment he was born again!

"Like newborn babies, you must crave pure spiritual milk so that you will grow into a full experience of salvation. Cry out for this nourishment"   1 Peter 2:2 NLT

In 1 Peter 2:2, Peter is writing to born-again Christians who have become new men in Christ. No one is born as a full-grown human being; we are born as babies in the natural, and then we grow up. Likewise, no one is born as a full-grown Christian. Christians are born as spiritual babies, and they grow up. No one thinks of a New baby as having a past, likewise, as someone who is Born A New, you do not have a past. You must grow by feeding on the Word of God.

God is saying: "You have become a new creature - a newborn baby! Your past is gone! I'm not remembering anything against you!" We are a brand-new creatures. We are a brand-new person. All that we were before we were born into the family of God is blotted out. We are God's children - His very own children.

Chapter 4

A New Leader

Walk in the Spirit, be led by the spirit.

> For they that are after the flesh do mind the things of the flesh; but they that are after the Spirit the things of the Spirit. For to be carnally minded *[is]* death; but to be spiritually minded *[is]* life and peace.   Romans 8:5-6

Under the New Covenant, every child of God has the Spirit of God. First, they are born of the Spirit. Then they can be filled with the Spirit. And they can expect to be led by the Spirit. For those of you who are new Christians, let me quickly explain these terms that many Christians talk about. Many times we Christians speak "Christianese" and don't realize that people do not understand our terminology.

To be **Born of the Spirit** means that the spirit of man is the part of man which is born again. The Christian's spirit has the life and nature of God in it. The inward man is born of God's Spirit and has the Spirit of God in him.

To be **Filled with that Spirit** means that the born-again Christian can be filled with that same Spirit which he already has in him. And when he is filled with that Spirit, there will be an overflowing of that Spirit. He will speak with other tongues as the Holy Spirit gives him utterance (Acts 2:4). He will have Power for witness and testimony. For more on this subject please see my book called "*Prophetic Grace – God's Set Time*".

To be **Led by the Spirit,** is what we will briefly talk about in this chapter. I wrote a whole section, in detail on following the Leadership of the Holy Spirit in this book; for now let us look at Romans chapter 8, it says "*For as many as are led by the Spirit of God, they are the sons of God.*" Even the born-again one who has not been filled with the Holy Spirit, has the Spirit of God abiding in him, and he can expect to be led and guided by the Holy Spirit.

> For if ye live after the flesh, ye shall die: but if ye **through the Spirit** do mortify the deeds of the body, ye shall live. For as many as are **led by the Spirit of God, they are the sons of God**. For ye have not received the spirit of bondage again to fear; but ye have received the Spirit of adoption, whereby we cry, Abba, Father. The Spirit itself beareth witness with our spirit, that we are the children of God: And if children, then heirs; heirs of God, and joint-heirs with Christ; if so be that we suffer with *[him]*, that we may be also glorified together. For I reckon that the sufferings of this present time *[are]* not worthy *[to be compared]* with the **glory which shall be revealed in us**. For the earnest expectation of the creature waiteth for the **manifestation of the sons of God**. For the creature was made subject to vanity, not willingly, but by reason of him who hath subjected *[the same]* in hope, Because the creature itself also shall be delivered from the bondage of corruption into the glorious **liberty of the children of God**. For we know that the whole creation groaneth and travaileth in pain together until now. And not only *[they]*, but ourselves also, which have the firstfruits of the Spirit, even we ourselves groan within ourselves, waiting for the adoption, *[to wit]*, the redemption of our body. Romans 8:13-23

True Sons (and Daughters) of God are led by the Spirit of God Who lives in their new heart. True Sons and daughters of God walk in Love and by the spirit mortify the deeds of the flesh. The Sons and Daughters of God desire to walk in Holiness.

> Therefore if any man be in Christ, he is a new creature: old things are passed away; behold, all things are become new. **2 Corinthians 5:17**

When we were born again, we died to our old nature. We now have the power of God's Spirit to mortify and put to death the desires of our flesh. Our spirits are brand new but we still have to put to death the selfish desires of the flesh. We still have to deal with our thoughts and temptations of the flesh.

As New Creations in Christ we now have a New Heart with a New spirit within us. We now also have a New Leader to follow, we no longer follow our selfish, carnal, fleshly temptations. Jesus is now the Lord of our lives, He is the Master and Ruler of our lives; He has final Word and Authority in our lives. Jesus has given us the Holy Spirit as our New Guide and Leader until He Comes again to Make all things New on this earth.

As our New Leader, the Holy Spirit in our New Born again spirit is trying to lead and guide us into the perfect will of God (John 16:13). As we have become Born-A-New, we now have the perfect leader within us to give us the advantage. It is up to us to choose to follow Him and Live this New Life.

We must put to death the desires of our flesh and instead let the New Man inside do the leading. We are now born of God.

> "Whosoever is born of God doth not commit sin; for his seed remaineth in him: and he cannot sin, because he is born of God" 1 John 3:9

The New Person on the inside of you is a New Creature, with the life and nature of God

A Christian's inward man isn't the one who wants to do wrong. If the inward man wants to do wrong, that person has never been born again.

First John 3:9 gives most Christians problems in understanding. Most have thought, If I were truly born of God, according to the Bible I wouldn't have sinned after I was saved. But this verse is talking about the inward man who doesn't sin.

Physically, we are born of human parents, and we partake of their human nature. Spiritually, we are born of God, and we partake of

His nature. And it is not God's nature to do wrong. Therefore, let your spirit dominate your flesh and resist the temptation to sin. I am born of God. My spirit has the life and nature of God, and its desires are right desires. With the Power of the Holy Spirit I have the Grace to not sin.

> "That which is born of the flesh is flesh; and that which is born of the Spirit is spirit. Marvel not that I said unto thee, Ye must be born again" John 3:6-7

If we have been born again than we are children of God. We are born of the Spirit of God. The Spirit of God leads us. He will lead us today. The Holy Spirit will rise big in us. He will bring illumination to our mind. He will give direction to our spirit. We can hear and be led by the Spirit of God.

Society has spent millions of dollars to develop the physical *body* of man. Additional millions have been spent developing man's intellectual processes, which are a part of his *soul.* But we know so little and have done so little about developing the *spirit* of man.

However, man's spirit can be educated and improved just as his mind can be educated and improved. The spirit can be trained and built up just as the body can be built up. How? Through the study of God's Word we can educate our minds as we educate and equip our spirit. As we become attentive to the Word of God our hearts receive faith and knowledge – God's Knowledge.

Our minds must be changed - renewed by God's power - for us to fully understand the Word of God. The Apostle Paul said,

> "But the natural man receiveth not [does not understand] the things of the Spirit of God: for they are foolishness unto him: neither can he know them, because they are spiritually discerned [under stood]" 1 Corinthians. 2:14

The Word of God was given by the Spirit of God, because"…holy men of God spake as they were moved by the Holy Ghost" (2 Peter 1:21). This is why the natural mind cannot understand God's Word. The Bible can only be understood with the heart. We must get the revelation of it in our spirit. Unless someone is born again they cannot see the Kingdom of Heaven. Unless someone is Born a New, they cannot receive the understanding and revelation of the Word of God that is imparted by the Holy Spirit of God.

Once a man is born again and becomes a child of God, he can understand the Bible and can learn spiritual things. As Paul said, he has become a new creature in Christ Jesus:

> "Therefore if any man be in Christ, he is a new creature: old things are passed away; behold, all things are become new" 2 Corinthians. 5:17

This process of renewing the mind with God's Word and receiving to heart the Word of God is a daily task: "…though our outward man perish, yet the inward man is renewed day by day" (2 Cor. 4:16).

The "inward man" is the real man, the real you. When the body dies, the inward man still lives. Paul said, "For to me to live is Christ, and to die is gain" (Phil. 1:21).

This does away with the theory that when a man is dead that is the end of him. It also does away with the theory of reincarnation, which teaches that after death a person can be born again in the world as a cow, a fly, a horse, a cat, etc… We need to stay with God's Word.

Why did Paul say that to die is gain? It surely is no gain to those of us who have lost loved ones, but it is gain for them. Paul went on to say,

> "For I am in a strait betwixt two, having a desire to depart, and to be with Christ; which is far better: Nevertheless to abide in the flesh is more needful for you" Philippians 1:23-24

The reason Paul said it was gain to die was because he would be with Christ in Heaven.

Chapter 5
A New School

Learn To Train Your Spirit

A key principle to following the inward witness is to develop and train your new spirit. Throughout our Christian walk we must try to do this as diligently as we can. The question is asked: "How do you train your spirit?" The answer to that question is to feed on God's Word. Jesus said,

> "Man shall not live by bread alone, but by every word that proceeds out of the mouth of God" Matthew 4:4

Another thing we must do is to make sure you we stay in love. We must make a quality decision that we are going to walk in love, regardless of whether or not anyone else does.

Another thing we can do is to pray much in other tongues. I know from experience that praying in other tongues is one of the best ways to build up your spirit man.

Too many of us spend most of our lives living in the mental and the physical realms. Many times we've developed our intellects instead of developing our hearts. When we do that, our intellects take the throne in our lives, and our spirits, which should guide us, are kept locked away in prison and are not permitted to function.

Whether or not we listen to our spirits, the Holy Spirit through the inward witness is always seeking to give guidance to our minds.

Let's learn to be sensitive to the Holy Spirit! Let's get to know the Leader who lives in us. I think many Christians have never really gotten acquainted with Him. They only know Him in a general sense, as if He is some sort of far-off God. But the Bible says the Holy Spirit is in us as our Comforter, Counselor, Helper, Intercessor, Advocate, Strengthener, and Standby (John 14:26 AMP).

If we will learn to let our spirit dominate our mind and flesh, then

"He will guide you into all truth, and He will show you things to come" John 16:13

Continue to school and train your spirit man to listen to the Holy Spirit who dwells inside you. Equip your Spirit and renew your mind with the Word of God and refuse to allow your flesh to dominate you. As you do, you will learn to follow the inward witness!

We know from the Word that a man's soul and spirit do not refer to the same thing because the Bible differentiates between them. It says,

"The word of God is quick, and powerful, and sharper than any two edged sword, piercing even to the DIVIDING ASUNDER of SOUL and SPIRIT." Hebrews 4:12

Actually, the Word of God teaches that you are a spirit, you have a soul, and you live in a body.

In Your Spirit
Since God dwells in you, in your heart (spirit), that is where He is going to speak to you. He does not communicate directly with your mind, because He's not in your mind; He's in your spirit.

You see, you are a spirit being, and you contact the spiritual realm with your spirit. You contact the mental realm with your intellect. And you contact the physical realm with your body.

It is your spirit that becomes a new creation in Christ when you are born again. When we are born anew, we still have the same body we had before. The outward man doesn't change. But the spirit man on the inside has become a new man in Christ. And because God guides us through our spirit, it's important to allow that inward man to dominate our lives.

Let me explain what I mean by the "inward witness." Suppose you pray about going in a certain direction in your life, and you get a check or a red light in your spirit. Or to say it another way, on the inside of you there is something that tells you no or to stop. On the inside, in your heart, you just don't feel peace, or good about going in the direction you're praying about.

That check in your spirit is the Holy Spirit telling you not to go in that direction, no matter how good circumstances look on the outside. On the other hand, if you pray about a matter and you get a go-ahead, green light signal or a peace, velvety-like feeling in your heart, that's the witness of the Holy Spirit telling you to proceed.

Various Ways
First, God leads His children by the inward witness. Second, He leads us by the inward voice. With the inward voice, our own spirit speaks to us what it picks up from the Holy Ghost. God also can lead us by the more authoritative Voice of the Holy Spirit. When the Holy Ghost within us speaks, it can almost seem to be an audible Voice.

You can't base your Christian walk on your physical senses or your feelings. Many times your feelings will tell you that you're not even saved!

Feeling is the voice of the body. Reason is the voice of your soul or mind. And conscience is the voice of your spirit. Your inward man has a voice; it is your conscience! Is your conscience a safe guide? It is if your spirit has been born again and your mind renewed by the Word of God.

If you are being led by your feelings or by your physical senses instead of by your conscience, you are heading for trouble and possibly danger. You contact this world with your physical senses. If your mind or body is dominating you, Satan can find entrance into your life and begin to control you through your feelings or senses.

You can't walk by faith if you're led by your emotions and feelings. It makes no difference whether or not you feel like something is so, or whether or not you feel like God heard you when you prayed. If the Word of God says it, then it's true!

"For the wages of sin is death; but the gift of God is eternal life through Jesus Christ our Lord" Romans 6:23

God contacts men through their spirits.

How can we experience the power of a new life found in our everyday walk with the Lord? The answer can be found in Romans 6:

"Therefore we are buried with him by baptism into death: that like as Christ was raised up from the dead by the glory of the Father, even so we also should walk in newness of life" Romans. 6:4

I want to draw your attention to the words *even so*. They mean the same thing as *just as*. Just as Jesus was raised up from the dead by the glory of the Father, so are we to walk in newness of life by that same glory. That glory is already in us. In spirit, we have already been resurrected to a level high enough to defeat anything the enemy would bring against us. The Father has enabled us as believers to live above the dominion of sin and death.

God has enabled us by giving us a new Heart, a reborn (born a new) spirit and filled us with His Spirit.

"A new heart also will I give you, and a new spirit will I put within you: and I will take away the stony heart out of your flesh, and I will give you an heart of flesh. And I will put my spirit within you, and cause you to walk in my statutes, and ye shall keep my judgments, and do them" Ezekial 36:26-27

Until we were born again and filled with His Spirit, we were held by the things of this natural world. We were dead to God and alive to sin.

Now, we have been crucified with Christ (Gal. 2:20). We have died to sin and have been raised together with Him (Eph. 2:5-6). The old sinner that we once were has died. We have become a new creation on the inside (2 Cor. 5:17).

A New Power

We experience the power of this new life by obeying the promptings of the Holy Spirit in our spirits. In order to serve God in this manner, we must give Him our full attention.

If you are not manifesting the power of God in your life, you don't need more of God, He needs more of you! If you keep Him shut out of your thoughts, then you will live a mere natural life. God wants your undivided attention so that you will learn to hear His voice.

When you hear His voice and obey His promptings, you will be sustained daily by the resurrection life that is in you through the Holy Spirit. He is in you to help you, strengthen you, teach you to mortify the deeds of the body, and lead you into all truth. He is your perfect Counselor.

Many people hear the Word of faith and decide that they will change their circumstances by speaking faith-filled words according to Mark 11:24. What many don't realize is that you can't fill your words with faith. Union with God through His Word fills your words with faith.

Words become faith words by hearing the Word of God. Really, by continually hearing and hearing and hearing, faith comes, and faith remains. If the world is distracting you from the Father, then most likely your "faith confessions" will be empty words.

You are not going to experience resurrection power unless you set your affection on Him. The promise of Mark 11:23-24 will still be yours, but it's conditional to your heart condition: "And shall not doubt in his heart, but shall believe...."

> Be not deceived; God is not mocked: for whatsoever a man soweth, that shall he also reap. For he that soweth to his flesh shall of the flesh reap corruption; but he that soweth to the Spirit shall of the Spirit reap life everlasting Galatians 6:7-8

If you want to reap the quality of life God has prepared for you, you must sow to the Spirit. It's just that simple. Sow the Word of God in your spirit and reap the benefits of the Word. Sow the Word of God into your spirit and see the benefits

What does the Scripture say? "...For the letter killeth, but the spirit giveth life" (2 Cor. 3:6). If we will concentrate on maintaining our union with the Father, our words will have authority. God's Spirit will make them alive with His power.

Sin, disobedience and living a selfish, carnal life will keep the life from flowing out. Romans 6:14 says that "sin shall not have dominion over you...."

You can't keep giving your attention to the things of this world and expect to get dominion over sin. As you set your affection on God and sow to the Spirit, a growing process will take place in you. You will be "changed from glory to glory as we behold the Lord, even by the Spirit of the Lord" (2 Cor. 3:17-18).

Then the Holy Spirit does the work in you, and you will begin to look more and more like Jesus. Sin will lose its hold on you. "This I say then, Walk in the Spirit, and ye shall not fulfill the lust of the flesh" (Gal. 5:16).

Isaiah 3:10 says, "Say ye to the righteous, that it shall be well with him: for they shall eat the fruit of their doings." If you do not live after your new nature of righteousness, then you will not eat the fruit of that righteousness. Verse 11 says "Woe unto the wicked! It shall be ill with him: for the reward of his hands shall be given him." This goes right along with Galatians 6:7-8, doesn't it?

Now look at Isaiah 59:

> Behold, the Lord's hand is not shortened, that it cannot save; neither his ear heavy, that it cannot hear: But your iniquities have separated between you and your God, and your sins have hid his face from you, that he will not hear. Isaiah 59:1

Sin separates you from the power of God even though you're born again. Resurrection life will lie dormant in you if you walk in sin. Until the flesh is brought into obedience by the Spirit, there is war waging in you. The flesh wants to dominate you, and the Spirit is endeavoring to suppress the flesh. But you can win that war!

> "This I say then, Walk in the Spirit, and ye shall not fulfill the lust of the flesh" Galatians 5:16

The way to overcome sin and the flesh is not to try and stop sinning. You dominate the flesh by walking after the new life that God put within you.

> "For ye are dead, and your life is hid with Christ in God" (Colossians 3:3).

> "Mortify therefore your members which are upon the earth [or, the flesh]" (v. 5).

> "And [you] have put on the new man, which is renewed in knowledge after the image of him that created him" (v. 10).

Walk after that inward man and your outward man will come into subjection to the Spirit. It takes knowledge of God, and knowledge of God comes by spending time in His Word and prayer.

Now, remember that our destination, or goal, is to be like Jesus. Romans tells us that we are predestinated to be conformed to His image (Romans 8:29).

How are we going to get there? Romans 8:1-2 tells us that it's going to be by walking after the quality of life we have received.

> "There is therefore now no condemnation to them which are in Christ Jesus, who walk not after the flesh, but after the Spirit. For the law of the Spirit of life in Christ Jesus hath made me free from the law of sin and death." Romans 8:1-2

We have enough of the resurrection life of God to walk in liberty while we are still on earth. We don't have to wait until we get to heaven for freedom from the law of sin and death. The life that is in Christ Jesus makes you free from that other law!

> "For what the law could not do, in that it was weak through the flesh, God sending his own Son in the likeness of sinful flesh, and for sin, condemned sin in the flesh: That the righteousness of the law might be fulfilled in us, who walk not after the flesh, but after the Spirit" Romans 8:3-4

The righteousness of the law is fulfilled in us as we walk not after the flesh, but after the Spirit.

> For they that are after the flesh do mind the things of the flesh; but they that are after the Spirit the things of the Spirit. For to be carnally minded is death; but to be spiritually minded is life and peace. Because the carnal mind is enmity against God: for it is not subject to the law of God, neither indeed can be. Romans 8:5-7

The Church will never have dominion over death as long as we are carnally minded. The spiritual mind brings forth life. A spiritual mind submits itself under the command of God, either by the written Word or by the inward witness of the Holy Spirit. The spiritual mind is open and ready to hear reproofs and corrections from the Spirit of God.

> But if the Spirit of him that raised up Jesus from the dead dwell in you, he that raised up Christ from the dead shall also quicken [make alive] your mortal bodies by his Spirit that dwelleth in you. Therefore, brethren, we are debtors, not to the flesh, to live after the flesh. For if ye live after the flesh, ye shall die: but if ye through the Spirit do mortify the deeds of the body, ye shall live. Romans 8:11-13

The Spirit of God is in us to raise us up from dead works. He will quicken our flesh. If we will give ourselves over to Him, resurrection life will dominate and subdue the flesh. The Holy Ghost subdues and quickens our mortal flesh. The life of God in us by the Spirit of God permeates outward.

We must allow the Holy Spirit to lead us in the everyday affairs of life and lead us into mortifying the deeds of the body.

If you don't know how to be led by the Spirit, make a decision to learn. Draw near to Him, and He will draw near to you. He will teach you. Tell the Lord, "I want to hear Your voice. I want to do what You tell me to do. I want to walk in Your resurrection power. I desire to experience the power to live a new life every day. By a decision of my heart, I put down the dictates of my flesh and mortify the deeds of the body. By the power of God, I receive a Holy Ghost refreshing in my life. In Jesus' Name!"

Chapter 6

A New Creation Reality

In the beginning, God..
God is the creator. In the Hebrew, the word for God is *Elohim*, which is God the Father, God the Son and God the Holy Spirit. The Name Elohim is plural, referring to the Trinity. In the beginning, the Bible says that God said "Let US make man in OUR image…"

In the beginning Christ had a major part in creating. In the following scriptures we see this: John 1:1-3 Col. 1:16 Eph. 3:9 1 Cor. 1:30 Proverbs 3:19 8:12-35. The Holy Spirit also had a major part as well: Gen. 1:2   Psa. 104:30.

The Trinity was also revealed in the New Testament (Matt 3:13-17 Matt. 28:19). The Trinity has been active, working together since the before the foundation of the world.

God and His Kingdom operates and function within laws that He created. A law is something that works every time (like gravity, seed time harvest, humility-pride). The law God used to create is the law of Faith. Words that we speak play a key role in God's Kingdom. (Psa. 8:2 Mark 11:22-23).

God reveals His Method of Operation.
God is a Faith God, and we are His children, His Family. We are a Family of Faith. God's method of Operation (M.O.) is speaking Faith Filled Words. God functions through words. (God said, and God saw). God always blesses through words (Gen. 1:22,28). Faith filled words have created everything around us.

Whatever is in your heart will come out of your mouth.The same process that got you born again is the same way you create your situation.(Rom. 10:9-10 Proverbs 4:20,23 Matthew 12:34-36   Luke 6:43-46). Like it or not, this principle is a law and it works weather we like it or not. What you believed and said from days before is what created your today. What you believe and say today will create your tomorrow. Our destiny is shaped by our heart and mouth.

Everything around us has been created by words.
Through faith we understand that the worlds were framed by the Word of God. (**Hebrews 11:3 Joshua 1:8**)*.* The word "FRAMED" means to put into words, to mutter, to utter and to conceive. It is similar to the word "meditate" in Joshua 1:8. The spirit realm is governed and ruled by words, by the law of faith.

God created everything. For us! (Genesis 1:14-15   Isaiah 45:18)

God created the heavens/universe for the earth. God created the earth because:

> **1)**. God desired with all His heart to have a Family. (a Family of Faith).
> **2)**. To provide a perfect home for His Family.
> **3)**. God wants all Mankind to be His Family. (**John 3:16**).

When God created the earth, He created it with everything that Man would ever need. God created Man because He desired to have relationship and fellowship.

We ARE significant! (Genesis 1:26-31 Gen. 2:7)

True significance is not measured by the world's perspective. Your significance is not measured by other people's opinions.
Significance is measured by Him who loves us, approves of us and our purpose for existence. Your performance has nothing to do with your significance in God's sight. (**Eph 1:6**)

You can't earn God's Love. The New Creation in Christ is a fulfillment of God's dream. You can't do anything to earn God's Love, you are loved because you exist. Man was created to live in unbroken fellowship and unending love relationship with God and each other (1 John 5:1-2), a family.

God giving Man the Earth

Man is to cultivate, keep, protect and guard what God has given Him. (**Genesis 2:8-17 Prov. 14:3 Prov. 18:20-21 Prov. 21:23**). God put man in Charge, He gave Him Authority.

God has made us New Creature's in Christ Jesus, the old things have gone and the new has come, and these new things are of God. Now lets look at God's original plan for Man, and how he fell and how all things are restored back in our redemption in Christ Jesus.

God's original plan for Man --DOMINION-- (Genesis 1:26-28 Psalms 8:4-6)

"Likeness" in the Hebrew means "exact duplicate in kind." "Image" in the Hebrew means "representative figure". Man was created a little lower than God (Elohim). The actual word for "angels" in Psa. 8:4-6 KJV is the same word used in Genesis chapter 1 for God.

God's class of being

The angels were in awe of what God created. (**Psa. 8:3-6**). They asked the question "what is man?" Then they answered their own question. Man was originally created a little lower then Elohim (God).Man was originally created to be like God. (with the same M.O.)

God crowns Man.

God crowns (clothes) Man with His Glory and Honor. All creatures have some kind of glory. (1 Corin. 15:40-41).Man was clothed with the Glory of God.

Authority is always accompanied with Responsibility.

Adams responsibility was to subdue the earth. (**Gen 1:28**). Adam also had to "keep" and cultivate his home, his life, the garden of Eden. Eden was a place of no lack, a place where all Adams needs were met. Eden is like a type of our place In Christ, where all our needs are met by God. "keep" in the Hebrew means to hedge about, to guard, to protect and to attend to. We "keep" our garden, our benefits in Christ is by our words.By speaking faith filled words we resist the serpent in our lives.

Satan's lie and the fall of Man. (Genesis 3:1)

The serpent was "crafty" and "subtle". Crafty and subtle means shrewd, cunning and skillful in deceiving. Satan's method of operation is deception and ignorance. Satan's presents a question "has God really said?" Satan twisted the truth to deceive Eve into thinking that she was not like God already. She was already in God's likeness and in His image.

She (like many Christians) didn't know who she was.Satan does not want you to know who you are in Christ. Satan wants to Steal, kill and destroy you, he tries to twists the truth to keep you ignorant of who you are in Christ. (**Romans 1:25**). Satan is terrified of Christians who know the truths of the Word of God concerning the New Creation and who they are In Christ. He does not want you to know all that the blood of Jesus has paid for. He does not want you to know what God has said concerning you. (**Eph. 4:18**)

God created Man as a spirit (a speaking spirit)
Adam and Eve were in Charge before they sinned. When they sinned they became spiritually dead and flesh led, they then lost the Glory of God. (**Rom**. 3:23-24)

Man's fall---Man's Redemption Through Christ.   (1 corin. 15:22)
Everyone born after Adam were born into Sin and death.
Dead men walking, (**Eph.2:1-10, Rom 5:12-18 1 John 5:19**) Sin separates us from God (**Isa. 59:2 Rom 3:23**). Everyone Born again is born into Life and Righteousness.When you were born again Eternal Life, Love and the Nature of God that Adam lost was put back.

Through our faith in the sacrifice of Jesus Christ on the cross we are justified , made righteous; **just-as-if-we'd-never-sinned**, we can act as though sin has never existed. Our sins have been erased, blotted out, remitted, cleansed and purged, never to remembered against you anymore (**1John 1:9 Isa. 43:25-26**)

When we are born again we are New Creations in Christ. (2 Corin. 5:17). A new creation is a new specous of being that had never existed before. What God did in the New Creation through Jesus Christ is far better than what Satan did to Adam. The New Creation is the most powerful thing God has created that is on the earth today.

God's rank of authority. (note: God puts His word higher than His name)
      1. God the Father, God the Son and God the Holy Spirit (Trinity).
      2. Born Again redeemed **Man In Christ- The New Creation**
      3. Angels of God
      4. Satan and fallen angels (demons)
      5. **Unsaved fallen Man**   (notice 2 families, God's and Satan's**)**

Rank of Authority scriptural references:
      1. Psa. 83:18   Eph. 1:20-22
      2. Eph 2:5-6 Psa. 8:4-6
      3. Hebrews 1:14 Psa. 103:20-21
      4. James 4:7 Luke 10:19

> 1Jo 5:4 For whatsoever is born of God **overcometh**- the world: and this is the victory that **overcometh**- the world, *even* our faith.
> 1Jo 5:5 Who is he that **overcometh**- the world, but he that believeth that Jesus is the Son of God?

Strong's biblical definitions: *overcometh=* to *subdue* (literally or figuratively): - conquer, overcome, prevail, get the victory.

In Christ Dominion is restored
The Bible is filled with New Creation Truths, and throughout this book you will learn about God's original plan for Man, and how he fell and how all things are restored back in our redemption in Christ Jesus. Now lets continue on our journey of the knowledge of God

and who we are in Christ. Jesus said that those who know the truth shall be set free.

Woman was deceived. (Genesis 2:15 + 3:1,6)
Woman was deceived with a question: "Has God really said?"Adam was not deceived, he willing disobeyed God. Adam knew the truth and had the authority from God to "keep" and "guard" the garden. Adam had the authority to kick the devil out of the garden. Being deceived is believing a lie.

After Adam and Eve fell (Gen. 3:9-14)
Their eyes were opened to evil.They recognized their nakedness for the first time. They lost the Glory of God. They lost Elohim's glorious image and likeness.

When Adam disobeyed God, Satan became his lord.
Adam transferred the authority God had given him. Through Adam's sin he gave his authority to Satan. (Luke 4:5-6   2 Cor. 4:4). God gave man free choice in whom he will serve.

At that moment of his disobedience Adams nature was changed
He was born from life to death. (Rom. 5:12-14). Adam and Eve died spiritually in the garden. (dead men walking). Death is separation from the Life of God, from God himself. (Eph. 4:18). Adam went from being a spirit ruled being to a sense ruled being. The natural (sense ruled) realm is limited, the spirit realm is limitless. Adam and Eve felt the hopelessness of being separated from God. (Eph. 2:12). Adam knew he couldn't reverse the consequences of sin. Adam didn't have 1 John 1:9. Everyone born after Adam is born with that same sin/death nature. (Romans 5:12-19).

Adam and Eve were separated and severed from God
Mankind is separated from the Life of God, from God Himself. (Eph 2:2-3. 12-13). God cannot cohabitate with sin. Selfishness became their ruling motive instead of love. They lost their significance. They tried to cover their nakedness. Sin brings *shame*, Sin brings *guilt*. Sin makes you want to *cover up* and *blame others* instead of taking responsibility. Sin brings *condemnation*, and condemnation makes you want to *run FROM* God.

Things that come into the world as a result of sin and death.
Fear, Guilt, shame, blame, condemnation and a Sin consciousness. A
sin nature that wants to sin (**Gen. 6:5**).

Sin Consciousness
Sin consciousness is identifying more with sin than righteousness.
Sin consciousness is the reason for every spiritual failure. It destroys
the initiative of the heart. It gives mankind an inferiority complex. It
brings a sense of unworthiness which destroys faith, mission and
vision (no vision and you will perish). It can rob us from our peace
of mind. It can cause the most zealous prayer life to become
ineffective and dead.

People will always try to ease their sin consciousness by Going to
church, fasting and doing penance or giving and doing all other
kinds of good works, being people pleasers. No works can relieve
you of sin consciousness. Only understanding the Righteousness of
God can get rid of a sin consciousness. Only eternal life (the Life of
God) can fill that void in a man's heart. Jesus gives that Life, He
gives that Righteousness. (**John 10:10 Rom.6:23 2 Cor. 5:21**)

Revelation of Righteousness and Grace (Eph. 2:8 John 6:63)
Once you are born again you are a New Creature, your spirit (your
heart) has become brand new. As we looked at in this book, when
you were born again you received: Eternal Life, the Love of God,
The Spirit of God, the Nature of God, the Faith of God, and all the
fruits of the spirit. You still have to deal with your flesh and your
mind.

You may be a New Creation but you still have to renew your mind
and develop a Righteousness consciousness. (Rom. 12:2 Eph. 4:24
Col. 3:10). Renew your mind to what the Word of God says about
you. Be mindful of what the Blood of Jesus has done (doing) for
you. He has remitted our sin.

Know and apply the truths of the Word of God, be doers of the Word
and not hearers only. Apply the fruit of the spirit so you can act like
God (Eph 5:1). The Word of God is able to restore your soul. (James

1:   ). God promises (peace) Shalom in our lives if we keep our minds on Him (Isa. 26:3).

See yourself as God sees you. *Develop a Righteousness consciousness.*

Meditate on these scriptures: Destroy sin consciousness
> **1. Col. 2:13-14   Heb. 10:10 Heb. 10:17-22   Philip. 3:9**
>
> **2. Rom. 8:1-4   1 Cor. 1:30   Eph. 1:6 Heb. 1:3 1 John 1:9**
>
> **3. 1 John 3:5 Rom. 3:24-25   2 Cor. 5:19-21   Matt. 26:27-28**

God doesn't remember your sins, so why should you? You are the righteousness of God, you are righteous! God imparted His own Righteousness to all that would believe on Jesus.

> **Righteousness** means: You can stand in the presence of a holy God without feelings of fear, guilt, shame and condemnation.

> **Justified** means: You have been declared Righteous, free from guilt and shame, declared innocent.

Righteousness restores what Adam lost. Righteousness causes you to stand fearless against the adversary. A righteousness consciousness gave Jesus the confidence to raise the dead. Righteousness gives you confidence in God's presence and in the presence of enemies and circumstances.

Now as we continue our study on who we are in Christ as New Creations we will look at our enemy and our position of authority over him. We will learn how to resist him and how not to let him into our lives, the Word of God says "to give No place to the devil" (Eph 4:27). As we learn we will not be ignorant of his devices and we can resist his attempts to gain access into our "garden". We will learn how to effectively "keep" our garden.

Ignorance is a powerful weapon. (Hosea 4:6)

The enemy keeps men captive through ignorance. The authority the enemy exercises against us is based on a lie. Satan fears the day you find out who you are and what belongs to you in Christ.

The bible tells us to be vigilant, sober and aware of the devil and his devices. The bible also tells us to not allow the devil to get access to our lives. The bible tells us all we need to know concerning Lucifer, the devil, Satan and his method of operation.

Here are his characteristics:
1. (**Gen.3:1**) the bible describes our enemy as ***subtle, clever, crafty and deceptive***. He fooled Eve.
2. (**1Peter 5:8**) Adversary the devil…..walketh about, ***seeking whom he may devour.***
3. (**John 10:10**) the thief cometh ***to steal, kill and destroy***
4. (**John8:44**) he is a ***murderer and a liar***.
5. (**Rev.12:10**) he is an ***accuser of the brethren*** …he accuses day and night.
6. (**Rev.12:9**) he is a ***deceiver of the world***.
7. (**2 Cor.11:4**) he can ***transform himself into angel of light***.
8. (**John 12:31; 14:30; 16:8,11**) he is called the ***prince of this world***. He has influence
9. (**Eph. 2:2**) he is called ***the prince of the power of the air, and he rules the spirit that works in the children of disobedience.***
10. (**2 Cor.4:4**) he is called ***the god of this world who blinds the mind so they won't come to believe.***

Satan is defeated by what God did at the cross of our Lord and Savior Jesus Christ.

Gen 3:15 (MSG) I'm declaring war between you and the Woman, between your offspring and hers. He'll wound your head, you'll wound his heel." (IN CRUCIFICTION THE HEEL IS BRUISED)

Heb 2:14 KJV Forasmuch then as the children are partakers of flesh and blood, he also himself likewise took part of the same; that through death he might destroy him that had the power of death, that is, the devil;

Strong's biblical definition: DESTROY in Heb. 2:14 to *be* (*render*) *entirely idle* (*useless*), - abolish, cease, deliver, destroy, do away, become (make) of no (none, without) effect, fail, bring (come) to nought, put away (down), vanish away, make void.

1Jo 3:8 KJV …. For this purpose the Son of God was manifested, that he might <u>destroy</u> the works of the devil.

1Jo 3:8 LITV ……For this the Son of God was revealed, that He might *<u>undo</u>* the works of the devil.

Strong's biblical definition: DESTROY in 1 John 3:8 to undo

Col.2:15NLT In this way, God disarmed and dethroned the evil rulers and authorities. He shamed them publicly by his victory over them on the cross of Christ.

Forbidden fruit (Genesis 2:15-17)
Don't open the door to the devil by partaking in the forbidden fruit (sin). Some (not all) of the forbidden fruit in the New Covenant are listed in the following scriptures: **1 Corin. 6:8-10 Rom. 1:26-28 Gal. 5:19-21 Eph. 5:11-12 Philip. 4:8**

Don't even allow this to be entertainment, Don't even speak of those things. Jesus said by looking at another in a lustful manor IS committing adultery in your heart; Likewise watching entertainment that has forbidden fruit is partaking in it.

Authority (James 4:7)

Authority means: "the right to command, the right to enforce obedience, lawful permission to execute power and the lawful permission to bring judgment or justice."
God has given you the authority to command. Adam had this authority but did not use it. The result of Adam not using this authority is the fall of man. Authority is delegated When you stick your hand up, its like God sticking His hand up. Jesus delegated His authority to us. (**Matt. 28:18**).

Jesus has given us ALL authority. (**Eph. 1:20-23**). Here are four things to remember when engaging the enemy Satan.

1. Jesus is the head and we are the body. (**Eph. 2:6**)
2. The throne of God is the seat of ALL authority.
3. You must identify yourself with the risen Christ, YOU are a throne sitter. (**Col. 3:1**)
4. YOU sit in heavenly places far above ALL things (**Eph. 1:17-22 Eph 2:6**).

There are two words for power. (**Luke 10:19**). Dunamis = power might and miraculous power and Exousia = delegated authority. An example: a police man's badge and his gun: his badge is the delegated authority from the city, his gun is the power to enforce against lawbreakers.

You received authority when you were born again, you receive the power when you receive the baptism in the Holy Spirit.

Power
Power for performing miracles. Dunamis = Dynamite. Scripture examples: Luke 1:35 Luke 4:14   Luke 24:49   Acts 1:8 Mark 5:25-30. The Gospel of Jesus Christ is the Power of God unto Salvation.

What is in a name?
All authority is enwrapped in the Name of Jesus. Using the name of Jesus gives us power of attorney (**Mark 16:15-18**). We must ask (demand) anything in His name and He will do it (**John 14:13**).

Strong's definition = "name" = (*authority*, *character*): - called, (+ sur-) name

Thayer Definition: "name" = the name is used for everything which the name covers, for one's rank, authority, interests, pleasure, command, excellences, deeds etc.

What does the name of Jesus mean?
Vine's dictionary says: **Jesus** is a transliteration of the Heb. "Joshua," meaning "Jehovah is salvation," or "is the Savior,"

BDB Hebrew dictionary says the name Jesus in the Hebrew is **Yeshuah** = Salvation, deliverance.
> **1a)** welfare, prosperity
> **1b)** deliverance
> **1c)** Salvation (by God)
> **1d)** victory

The Strong's biblical definition **of the word for Salvation =** *rescue* or *safety* (physically or morally): - deliver, health, save, saving.

God said in His Word that "My people are destroyed because of a lack of knowledge" and Jesus said "Ye shall know the Truth and the Truth shall set you free". As we renew our mind and receive the seed of the Word of God in our hearts; Our image of ourselves will change and we will have the mind of Christ and not the mind of the world or religion. Praise God for His Word which is the Final Authority in life.

Our Authority comes from knowing who you are and what is yours. Authority doesn't come from volume; how loud you speak. Satan fears the day you find out who you are. (**Luke 7:28**). Authority is delegated to every believer.

We have been given the authority to bind and loose. (Matt. 16:19 Matt. 18:18)

What you bind (forbid) on earth is forbidden in heaven. What you loose (permit) on earth is permitted in heaven. The initiative rests with you.

Jesus' Authority (Matt. 8:5-11)

Speak the word only. The centurion recognized Jesus as having authority over sickness and disease. You have authority over sickness and disease

Renewing the mind

Your spirit was recreated but your soul needs to be renewed. What a man thinks is what he is (**Prov. 23:7**). We must have a Righteousness consciousness. See yourself as a Joint Heir with Christ, like God (**Philip. 2:4-11 Psa. 8:4-6**). As we learn and meditate on who we are in Christ, we will renew our mind from "stinkin thinking" and we will gain a greater image of who we are in Christ and what he has given us freely. The Holy Spirit will help us (**1 Corin. 2:12**).

Story of Moses sending out the 12 spies. (Numbers 13)

10 spies came with a bad report and 2 came with a good report. (**Num. 13:31-33**). 10 spies saw themselves as grasshoppers. 2 spies saw themselves as God saw them. they all had what they said (**read numbers 14:28 37-38**). The 10 (and all who agreed with them) did not enter in to the promised land; and the 2 (and all who agreed with them) entered into the promised land. (**Heb. 3:18**). Our promised Land is: All the rights and privileges in Christ (enjoying them). We enter in by believing the good report of the Word of God concerning who we are in Christ. Their thinking determined their destiny. See yourself as God sees you "More than a conqueror" .

We have to renew our mind to think and see like God.

The Israelites were robbed of the promises of God because of what they thought and said. Joshua and Caleb believed God in spite of the giants. God said that Joshua and Caleb had a different spirit than the rest of the congregation. Think on things that are of God (**Philip. 4:8**). You have to enlarge your mind (your thinking) with the word of God. Always remember these four things and never allow limits to be put on you and your God.

1. With God all things are possible.
2. All things are possible to those who believe.
3. Is anything too hard for God
4. You and God make the majority.

God wants to remold you. (Rom. 12:2)
Don't let the world squeeze you into its mold. Let God remold you by allowing the Word of God to wash through you. The world wants to dictate what you can do and who you are.

God's Word as a mirror (James 1:23-25)
Wrong thoughts will distort your image. The Word of God is the correct image. There are 3 things that you have to do with the mirror (Word of God).

1. Look intently.
2. Must abide in front of the mirror.
3. Must be an effectual doer of the Word.

We are transfigured in ever increasing degrees. (**2 Cor. 3:18 AMP**). The worst thing that you can do is walk away from the mirror (WORD) before you look at yourself and see yourself as the mirror (WORD) sees you.

Thoughts - Strongholds (2 Cor. 10:4-5)
Strongholds are speculations, theories, reasoning's, proud arguments or deceptive fantasies. Strongholds attempt to talk you out of what God has promised you. Strongholds try to keep the unsaved from coming to Christ, and try to stop the Christian from having God's best for their lives. Strongholds are thieves and we must do something about them. Here are five things you must do:

1. Identify the thief.
2. Arrest the thief and put a stop to him.
3. Pronounce judgment on the thief.
4. Sentence the thief and rehabilitate your mind.
5. Take the Word of God wherever you go and rehabilitate those thoughts, destroy those strongholds.

Overcome strongholds with the Word of God. By meditating, speaking, listening and thinking the Word of God.

Chapter 7

A New Love

When we are born again and become New Creations in Christ we receive a new nature; We pass from death to life, our hearts are changed. The Bible says we receive the Love of God, the Faith of God and all the fruits of the Spirit. We do not receive the spirit of fear; but we Do receive the Spirit of Power and of Love and of a sound mind. In this chapter we will look at our New nature, our new heart and allow our New heart from God to lead us.

We have the Love of God (Rom.5:5)
Allow the Love of God to govern your life. **The God-kind of love is not human. (John 3:16**). His love is supernatural and "Holy Spirit-injected."

The human kind of love is conditional. God's love is unconditional. When you become born again, the Holy Spirit "injects," or pours, God's love into your heart (**Romans 5:5, *AMP***). Loving others is proof that you are born again.
You must love others even when it's not easy to do so.
Your love walk must be based on what the Word of God says, even when it instructs you to love others in unconventional ways.

> **Matthew 5:43-44**: "*Ye have heard that it hath been said, Thou shalt love thy neighbour, and hate thine enemy. But I say unto you, Love your enemies, bless them that curse you, do good to them that hate you, and pray for them which despitefully use you, and persecute you.*"

Ask the Holy Spirit to help you. Loving others even when it hurts positions you to live the "too much" lifestyle-a life of too much favor, anointing, wealth, goodness and health. Love will quench the spirit of strife. Make it a point to greet those who dislike you with a hug, a kiss or with words that will edify them. God's love in you will compel your enemies to constantly seek after you. They will want to be in contact with that love. Don't allow the fear of rejection to stop you from loving anyone.

The love of God is His power.
You receive *power*-ability, efficiency and might-the moment the Holy Spirit takes up residence within your born-again spirit (**Acts 1:8, *AMP***).

You receive an endowment of power enabling you to do anything. Love is the power that you receive (**Romans 5:5, *AMP***). Love demands a positive change in how you relate to others. God (Love) is able to do exceeding, abundantly and above all that you could ever ask or think *according* to the love that is at work in you (**Ephesians 3:20**).

Others will recognize that you belong to God because of your love walk. The level of excess and abundance you experience will be determined by the love that is at work in you. Living a life of love will give you access to heaven and enable God to recognize you as His.

Recognize that the Greater One (Love) lives in you (1 John 4:4).
Love (God) is a "nuclear weapon" against forces, because darkness cannot gain the upper hand when love is in control of your life. As you perfect your love walk, make plans to receive your end-time harvest.

You experience immediate and positive results when you are quick to cultivate the love of God. Without love, you are a "useless nobody" (**1 Corinthians 13:1-2, *AMP***).
Cultivating the *gifts* of the Spirit is not as important as cultivating the *fruit* of the Spirit-love. Love is the master key to unlocking the things of God.

Walking in love is profitable. (1 Tim 4:7-8)
Walking in love is godliness. To exercise at something means to make it a practice, or to work at something, to make it a way of life. When we work on walking in love we are exercising love and godliness the Bible says that it is profitable unto all things.

Walking in love causes us to inherit a blessing. (1 Peter 3:8-10 Luke 6:35-38). Walking in love is not rendering evil for evil, instead when we walk in love we bless; knowing that when we do we will inherit a blessing. That's why Jesus told us to love our enemies, bless them, pray blessings upon them, do good to and for them.

Controlling your tongue is part of walking in love. (1 Peter 3:10-14)

In these scriptures we see that if we control our tongue we will see "good days". Love always refrains from talking evil. Love speaks no guile or evil about others. The God kind of Love seeks peace with every person. God will not allow anyone to harm you as you walk in love.

God's Love never fails.

1 Cor. 13:4-8
Love is patient and kind.
Love knows neither envy nor jealousy.
Love is not forward and self–assertive, nor boastful and conceited.
Love does not behave unbecomingly, nor seek to aggrandize herself, nor blaze out in passionate anger, nor brood over wrongs.
Love finds no pleasure in injustice done to others, but joyfully sides with the truth.
Love knows how to be silent. She is full of trust, full of hope, full of patient endurance.
Love never fails….

God's Love never fails! Therefore, if you are walking in His divine Love, **You CANNOT FAIL**.

Overcome evil with good. If you are walking in the God-kind of Love, His Love working in and through you will be more than enough for any situation. The God-kind of love will put you over in life because God is Love. When you walk in the God-kind of Love you cannot be defeated. You are born of God (who is Love) you are a overcomer. (**1 John 4:4 1 John 5:1-5).**

The number one objective for every Christian should be to become like Christ. The only way to do this is to perfect the love of God in your life.

Love is a commandment, not an option (John 15:12).
The love of God is not a human type of love, but a supernatural kind of love. It is not conditional. You know you have crossed from death to life by the love you bear for others (**John 13:34-35**). If you don't love others, you are still spiritually dead. (**1 John 3:14-15).** You can't be born again and hate others.

Walking in the love of God is a huge part of the Christian lifestyle; everything depends on it: The proper working of your faith. The manifestation of the gifts of the Spirit and the promises of God. The degree to which God can work through you and on your behalf.

As you perfect your love walk, you perfect everything that concerns you. Perfected love casts out fear. Believers should not fear. God wants you to love fervently, with a pure heart (**1 Thessalonians 3:12**). He wants your love to be unfeigned-not false (**1 Peter 1:22**). Selfishness is a force that works against the love of God. You cannot profit without love. (**1 Tim. 4:8**) godliness is walking in Love

The love of God is not selfish or self-seeking (1 Corinthians 10:33, 13:5-7).
Love gives, lust takes. Lust is simply defined as "satisfying itself at the expense of others" Love, on the other hand satisfies others at the expense of itself". If you are more concerned about fulfilling your own desires than fulfilling the desires of others, you are not walking in love.

A good example is when husbands or wives who insist that their spouses purchase a particular item when they know they cannot afford it.Selfishness always breeds hypocrisy. Don't just say "I love you" and pass up the opportunity to minister to someone.

Selfishness is obsessed with self-preservation. Fear keeps you afraid of running out resulting in being stingy and greedy. Faith keeps you confident that you have abundance; resulting in a loving and giving heart. Prosperity is being able to bless someone else. Become possessed by the spirit of love and put others first **(Philip. 2:2-4)**

Love is not touchy or easily provoked (1 Corinthians 13:5).
Love does not take offense. Love doesn't say something that injures another person.

Love does not take account of the wrong done to it; it pays no attention to a suffered wrong (1 Corinthians 13:5).
Love does not keep a record of offenses. Love does not bring up past sins or mistakes. Love is quick to forgive. Love always forgives.

Love does not rejoice at injustice or unrighteousness (1 Corinthians 13:6).

Love bears up under everything; it bears all things (1 Corinthians 13:7).
Love covers with silence; it protects people. It never uncovers scandal or reveals the flaws of others. Love never fails.

Experiencing the miracle of the new birth makes you a partaker of eternal life. Heaven becomes your destination when you die. But the new birth is much more than a ticket to heaven. It also carries with it some wonderful benefits in this life as well.

Let's look at three major changes that result from being born again:

A New Species of Being
According to the Word of God, the remaking of your spirit makes you a whole new type of being.

> "Therefore if any man be in Christ, he is a new creature: old things are passed away; behold, all things are become new." (2 Cor. 5:17)

When you are born again, the things that characterized your old lifestyle - your old habits, priorities and ways of talking - pass away. You no longer have to be controlled by the things of your past. You're free!

Down through the centuries, "religious" people have demanded that "sinners" clean up their lives before they come into the church. Many an unsaved person has been told, "Purify your life, then you can be a Christian." According to the Word of God, that is completely out of sequence. A person has no ability to make lasting changes in his lifestyle until he's been made a new creation in Christ Jesus.

Becoming a new creature is what makes it possible for all old things to pass away and all things to become new. Your marriage can become new. Your relationships with your children can become new. Everything becomes new because YOU are a new person!

This new personhood calls for a new way of thinking. Rom. 12:2 calls it "renewing your mind." It means retraining your mind to realize that you don't have to be sick anymore. You don't have to be poor anymore. You no longer have to be defeated. The world may have to live that way, but not you - you're a new creation!

All Things Are Now Possible

"...all things are possible to him that believeth." (Mark 9:23)

It takes an act of "believing" to be born again and as a "believer" nothing is impossible to you. In fact, as a child of God, you can overcome anything the devil or the world can throw at you.

"For whatever is born of God over cometh the world." (1 John 5:4)

"...we are more than conquerors through him that loved us." (Rom. 8:37)

When you've been born again you're not just a survivor, you're not just a conqueror, you're MORE than a conqueror through Jesus!

Your Needs Are Now Abundantly Supplied

One of the most comforting and exhilarating aspects of the new birth is the knowledge that everything you need has been supplied in advance.

If you need healing, 1 Peter 2:24 says, "By whose stripes ye were healed." In other words Jesus bore your sickness and pain on the cross. You don't have to be sick anymore.

If you have financial needs, Philippians 4:19 says "But my God shall supply all your needs according to his riches in glory by Christ Jesus."

That didn't say some of your needs. It didn't say most of your needs. God's Word says all of your needs are met in accordance with His amazing heavenly abundance.

These are just a few of the marvelous benefits that belong to the born-again child of God.

Three Keys to Enjoying the Fullness of the New Birth

A vast majority of Christians are "living beneath their privileges." What do I mean by that? I'm referring to the fact that as born-again believers we have inherited enormous rights and privileges. We're children of the King!

Yet far too many believers are content to trudge through life like lowly beggars, consoling themselves in the knowledge that they'll go to heaven by and by.

You don't have to live that way. Jesus said He came to bring you abundant life. The following three keys will help you appropriate all the benefits the new birth brings.

1. Unlocking God's Promises

God's Word is literally filled with promises to you, as a believer. However, those great and precious promises will not become a reality in your life automatically. You must unlock them with the key of faith.

Yes, to receive the fullness of God's promises in your life you must have faith, and the only source of faith is the Word of God.

"So then faith cometh by hearing, and hearing by the Word of God." (Rom. 10:17)

When you focus your time and attention on God's Word, faith is the result. I'm talking about the kind of faith that will bring God's promises down from the realm of the spirit right into your life.

We get a glimpse of how faith works in Hebrews 11:1:

"Now faith is the substance of things hoped for..."

When you first read a promise in God's Word, it enters your mind as "hope." This begins the process of faith. Then as you meditate on that promise and confess it over your situation (saying what God's Word says about it), hope drops down into your heart and becomes faith.

2. Understand the Enemy of Your Faith

In discovering the wonderful truth about faith don't make the mistake of thinking all your problems will instantly vanish the moment you are born again. Many new Christians see God's promises in the Bible and assume they can simply float around on a "faith cloud."

The Bible, however, makes it very clear that we have a real enemy to contend with in this life:

"Be sober, be vigilant; because your adversary the devil, as a roaring lion, walketh about, seeking whom he may devour:" (1 Peter 5:8)

Satan will try to come against you with sickness, oppression and poverty - the very things Jesus died to redeem you from. But if you'll refuse to listen to his lies and stand firm on God's Word, you'll rise above every circumstance.

The most important thing a new believer needs to be aware of is that Satan's favorite and most insidious tactic is to steal the Word from your heart. Jesus exposed this method in the parable of the sower and the seed:

"When any one heareth the word of the kingdom, and understandeth it not, then cometh the wicked one, and catcheth away that which was sown in his heart." (Matt. 13:18,19)

It is vital that new believers recognize that they have an enemy who is out to steal the Word from their hearts.

3. Be Built Up in God's Word
There is a reason Satan is so determined to steal the Word before it can take root in your heart. That Word will cause you to grow in power, faith and authority.

"As newborn babes, desire the sincere milk of the word, that ye may grow by it." (1 Peter 2:2)

In this respect, a brand new Christian is no different than a newborn baby. Both must eat in order to grow and gain strength.

Once your spiritual growth and development begins, the new life that is yours in Christ through faith will begin to open to you. Before long the memory of your old life will begin to seem like nothing more than a bad dream. You'll wonder how you could have ever lived without the joy that is available to you through the new birth.

Just be sure to be diligent in your study of God's Word. It's your source of spiritual nourishment.

Getting it Settled
If you've never been born again or if you have some questions in

your mind concerning your relationship with Jesus Christ, you're only a prayer away from settling those issues once and for all. Take a moment to pray this prayer. Say the words from your heart. If you mean them, Jesus will come into your heart and you will be born again:

God in Heaven, I come to you in the name of Your Son, Jesus. I confess that I haven't lived my life for You. I believe that Jesus is the Son of God. I believe that He died on the cross and rose again from the dead so I might have a better life now and eternal life in heaven. Jesus, come into my heart and be my Lord and Savior. From this day forward, I'll live my life for You to the best of my ability. In Jesus' name I pray, Amen.

Now thank God for saving you and know for sure your life will never be the same again.

Three kinds of Love.

- **Agape -** The God-Kind of Love. It is not based upon feelings but upon the will. It is expressed in total obedience to God's commands. Agape willingly denies it self for the betterment of others. Its primary objective is God. (**1 John 5:3 and John 15:13**)

- **Phileo -** Brotherly love or human love. Phileo is based on feelings and can soon come to an end. It is conditional love and will only operate when there is feelings or affinity for others. (**John 21:15 Amp**)

- **Eros -** Based upon self-gratification and physical desire. Patience is not an element of eros. Eros is five-senses oriented, and is always at the expense of others. (**2 Samuel 11:1-4**)

Chapter 8
A New Character

- **Joy** - as a fruit of the Spirit, joy is eternal. Joy is strength! It is contrasted with natural joy (which is based upon natural circumstances and is temporary). (**Nehemiah 8:10**)

- **Peace** - The Amplified Bible defines the fruit of peace as "that tranquil state of a soul assured of its salvation through Christ, and so fearing nothing from God and content with its earthly lot of whatever sort that it is." (**Philippians 4:7**)

- **Long-suffering (Patience)** - Endurance and steadfastness under trial. It is an even temper and forbearance. (**James 1:3-4**)

- **Gentleness** - Strength under perfect control. It can be compared to a mother nursing and cherishing her young or how a husband should be to his wife. (**I Thessalonians 2:7 Amp Ephesians 5:29**)

- **Goodness** - The Greek word for goodness is *agathoosune* which means a state of being good, kind, benevolent, generous and God-like in life and conduct. (**Galatians 5:22**)

- **Faithfulness** - Reliable, trustworthy, dependability and being ever true to promises. (**Matt. 25:20-21 I Corin. 1:9 Amp.**)

- **Meekness** - A state of being in which one is totally dependent upon God, being mild, forbearing, submissive and humble. (**James 1:21 Amp.**)

- **Temperance (self-control)** - Self-restraint of impulses, emotions or desires; inward strength. (**I Corin. 9:24-27**)

One of the purposes of this book is to impart life changing revelation and insight into the character and nature of Jesus which can be found in all nine Fruit of the Spirit that were imparted into our lives when we were born again. In this chapter we will learn how to cultivate and develop these fruits and in turn will develop in character and grow spiritually mature. Our goal is to be formed into the image and likeness of Jesus Christ.

"Sons" in Romans 8 is the Greek word *uihos (hwee-os)* is a word that means to be in the same character and nature as the Father. God has already placed the qualities of the Fruit of the Spirit in you. (**Romans 5:5**). We have to develop each fruit, each part that makes up true Christian character. Only that can carry the anointing, power and gifts of the Holy Ghost. (**1 Corin. 13:13**). We must practice at developing these fruits of the Spirit.

Without the fruits of the Spirit the Gifts of the Spirit will not last. Walking in the Spirit as a Christian is going to take an act of your will. Salvation is a choice and walking in the fruit of the Spirit is a choice. If the world doesn't see the Fruit of the Spirit in our lives, we will be labeled as hypocrites and phonies.

How Jesus is formed in the believer

The nine fruit (outward manifestation of character) of the Spirit is found in Galatians 5:22. It is Love, Joy, Peace, Longsuffering, Gentleness, Goodness, Faith (faithfulness), Meekness and Temperance

Jesus is formed in the life of the believer (Galatians 4:19). The fruit of the Spirit forms and molds us into the image and likeness of Jesus Christ. Jesus' desire is to be seen in your life. The fruit of the Spirit that manifests in the life of the believer gives Him the opportunity to be seen. (**John 3:30 Romans 8:29**). As we grow and develop in the fruit of the Spirit, people will see less of us and more of Jesus.

Chapter 9
Developing character

Love
- Never fails. (I Corin. 13:8)
- Takes no action of a suffered wrong. (I Cor. 13:5)

Joy
- Strengthens us in trials and persecution. (Matt. 5:11-12 James 1:2)
- Works like a medicine, bringing healing. (Prov. 17:22)

Peace
- Acts as an umpire in our hearts. (Col. 3:15 Amp.)
- Garrisons and mounts guard over our hearts and minds. (Philip. 4:7 Amp.)

Patience
- Enables us to obtain the promises of God. (Hebrews 6:12 James 1:4)
- Causes us to run the race set before us. (Hebrews 12:1)

Gentleness
- Acts with courtesy towards opponents. (2 Tim. 2:25 Amp)
- Causes us to share our lives with others. (1 Thess. 2:8 Amp.)

Goodness
- Like salt, acts as a preservative in society. (Matt. 5:13)
- Glorifies God in the presence of unbelievers. (1 Peter 2:12)

Faithfulness
- A key to true promotion. (Matt. 25:20-21)
- Loyal to the truth. (3 John 3-5)

Meekness
- Does not retaliate, leaves vengeance to God. (Numbers 12:1-13)
- Accepts and obeys the implanted Word. (James 1:21-22)

Self-control

- Causes us to receive the crown of eternal blessedness. (1 Corin. 9:25 Amp.)
- Causes us to be better than he who takes a city. (Proverbs 16:32)

The development of our Character

God is looking for a person who will look, walk, talk, and act like Jesus in the earth.

We would be a lot more effective if we knew what God knew and understood what God understood. We have to choose between being carnally minded and spiritually minded.

God is not impressed with how we act in front of people; He wants you to act the same all the time. There is a law of association and character. (**Prov.13:20**)

Spanish proverb: "Tell me who you go with and I'll tell you who you are." Bad company corrupts good morals. ( ). You can influence others without them influencing you. If you hang around people that complain and you don't guard yourself you will become a complainer as well.

By spending time with people that have developed the fruit of the Spirit will help you grow in the fruit of the Spirit. You become like those you associate with, associating with God will cause you to be like God.

It is important to take account of your personal association. You are greatly affected by the people you associate with. **Proverbs 13:20 -** he that walks with wise men shall be wise. A great man of God, Dr. Jerry Savelle, says: "Association means: frequently in the company of; combined resources for a common goal."

How the fruit of the Spirit matures the believer.

Believers would often choose the Gifts of the Spirit rather than the fruit of the Spirit. God wants us to have both, we don't have to choose one or the other. Walking in the Spirit and with the fruit of the Spirit will protect the anointing and gifts on your life. By following the call to have both the Gifts and the Fruit of the Spirit, the Church will experience:

> **a**. Unity of the faith
> **b**. Maturity
> **c**. Stability
> **d**. Demonstration of the fullness of Christ.

A Full Gospel Church demonstrates Jesus in His fullness. (**Colossians 2:9-10**). The mature, balanced Church operates in full capacity in both the Fruit and the Gifts of the Spirit. The Fruit of the Spirit is the foundation for the power gifts.

Balance
There must be balance of the Fruit and Gifts of the Spirit. I Corin. 12 = talks about the Gifts of the Spirit. I Corin. 13 = talks about the fruit of the Spirit; Love. I Corin. 14 = talks about the Gifts of the Spirit. We need to have both; the Fruit and the Gifts.

Churches have placed greater emphasis on the Gifts of the Spirit. In order to mature there must be an equal emphasis placed on the Fruit of the Spirit. A Church with Gifts and no Fruit is a Church filled with characters. A Church with Gifts and Fruit is a Church with character.

To walk in the Spirit (Galatians 5:16,25)
To live in the Spirit is one thing but to walk in the Spirit is another. The world will be blessed when we make the choice to walk in the Spirit. When we allow the Fruit of the Spirit to manifest in our lives we will find out that God will cause us to walk down paths that we never dreamed of.

We are saved by Grace but it is our responsibility to grow up into the things that God has for us. Willingness and obedience will cause you to grow and increase. Don't mistake your emotions for faith. You can tell you are in faith when you are being motivated by what

God's Word says. You can tell you are operating by your emotions if you are being motivated by what your flesh wants.

When it comes to walking in the Spirit you must do it by faith. To walk in Love, Joy, Peace, Patience, Goodness, Faithfulness, Meekness and Temperance is to walk in the Spirit. Walking in the Spirit will prevent the believer from walking in the flesh.

The Fruit of the Spirit glorifies the Father
John 15:8 says: "The Father is glorified when you bare much fruit". The Father is glorified when He sees His sons and daughters operating in the Fruit of the Spirit. If we are going to bare much fruit we must abide in Jesus the Vine.

Matthew 5:16   Romans 8:6
We are told to" Let your light shine before men." We don't walk in the Spirit on God's account.If you remain attached to the root source (God, Jesus, Holy Ghost) you will bare much fruit.

Abiding in the Vine = being vitally connected to Jesus, If you abide in the Vine you will bare much fruit. You will never come up short in the fruit of the Spirit.be connected to the Vine and it will supply any need you have.

How the Fruit of the Spirit proves the ministers of God.
2 Corin. 6:3-6 - "Give no offense that your ministry be not blamed."True men and women of God are not discerned by the Gifts of the Spirit, but rather by the Fruit of the Spirit.

Matthew 7:15-20 " …you shall know them by their fruits…"

Someone once said: "Those who exercise spiritual gifts have the greatest need to show the Fruit of the Spirit. There is real power in the Fruit of the Spirit. It is the quiet influence of a beautiful life, rather than the rushing power of a fiery ministry, and it comes from communion."

Abiding in the Vine comes by communion with the Father.

The quality decision in relation to the Fruit of the Spirit
The fruit of the Spirit is developed by a quality decision. Joshua 24:15 - " .. as for me and my household we will serve the Lord."

You know someone has made a quality decision when they follow through with their decision for the rest of their lives.

Definition of a quality decision: A decision that is based in the authority, integrity and revelation of God's Word. It is a firm decision that cannot be reversed. Time will always prove if you have made a quality decision or not.Walking in the Spirit is always a choice.

Fruit of the Spirit is cultivated
The seed is on the inside, but there needs to be a cultivation process to cause it to grow to its fullness(**Philippians 2:12-15**).

Developing the nine Fruit of the Spirit is a spiritual exercise or a spiritual workout. A spiritual workout is to cultivate or to carry out the goal. A spiritual workout is not for earning salvation.

We cultivate the Fruit of the Spirit by:

> **1**. Praying in the Spirit. (**Jude 20**)
> **2**. Meditating the Word of God. (**Psalms 119:11**)
> **3**. Carrying out quality decisions. (**Philippians 3:12-14**)

2 Peter 1:3-10
Conditions helpful to Fruit bearing.
God decreed that man should be fruitful and multiply. (**Gen. 1:28**). God decreed Man to be fruitful over Adam and Eve, Noah, Abraham (Gen. 17:6), Jacob and Joseph.

It is very important that we do not give place to offenses and unforgiveness. (**Mark 6:3-6**). Offense is a spiritual force. The offense of the people in Jesus' hometown, hindered Jesus from performing mighty miracles. Protecting ourselves from an overcrowded heart. (**Mark 4:18-19**). We must learn from the parable of the sower. The Word can get choked out by outside circumstances.

Godly Associations (Ephesians 5:9-11). Don't associate with darkness. Proverbs 27:17 "Iron sharpens Iron"

When we walk in obedience, everything in our lives has to yield to increase and fruitfulness. Isaac was obedient and fruitful in the time of famine and he reaped a 100 fold.

The fruit of Love
The fruit broken down into three sections (**Galatians 5:22-23**)

1. Love, Joy and Peace = deals directly with God, can only come with a relationship with God.
2. Longsuffering (Patience), Kindness and Goodness = Always deals with other people.
3. Faithfulness, Gentleness (Meekness) and self control = Inward qualities

Definitions of Love: God IS Love. (**I John 4:8**). Love always gives of itself (**John 3:16**)

1. Love cannot only be verbally said but it has to be shown.

2. Love gives at the expense of self for the benefit of others.

3. Love is the fountainhead of all other fruit. (**I Corin. 13:1-3**)

The Dynamics of Love

Love is either fed or starved by words. Faith works by Love. (**Galatians 5:6**). The effective operation of our faith is dependent on walking in Love. Quote from **Kenneth Hagin, Jr.** - "If we aren't walking in Love, our faith won't work! As we study the Fruit of the Spirit, we find that we cannot have any of the Fruit of the Spirit in operation until we have Love."

The enemies of Love (1 Corin. 13:4-6)

Envy - A feeling of discontent or ill will due to another's advantages, possessions, or successes. Envy is the chief source of division in the Body of Christ.

Other enemies of love are: Pride, Arrogance (puffed up), Rude behavior, self seeking, being easily provoked, evil thinking, rejoicing in iniquity.

Proverbs 20:3 "it is to a man's honor to avoid strife"

Chapter 10

New Fruit

Developing character: The fruit of the Spirit

Characteristics of Love according to I Corinthians 13:4-8 Amp.

- **Love** endures long, is patient and kind.

- **Love** is never envious nor boils over with jealousy

- **Love** is not boastful or vainglorious.

- **Love** does not display itself haughtily.

- **Love** is not conceited, arrogant or inflated with pride.

- **Love** is not rude or unmannerly and does not act unbecoming.

- **Love** (God's Love in us) does not insist on its own rights or its own way, for it is not self-seeking.

- **Love** is not touchy, fretful or resentful.

- **Love** takes no account of the evil done to it and pays no attention to a suffered wrong.

- **Love** does not rejoice at injustice and unrighteousness, but rejoices when right and truth prevails.

- **Love** bears up under anything and everything that comes.

- **Love** is ever ready to believe the best of every person.

- **Love's** hopes are fadeless under all circumstances and it endures everything without weakening.

- **Love** never fails, fades, becomes obsolete nor comes to an end.

The Fruit of Joy (Galatians 5:22)
Qualities of Joy.
The Power to overcome is Joy's main attribute. Other words for Joy - gladness, delight, rejoice, satisfaction and blessedness. Joy is the energy of the Holy Spirit, "The Joy of the Lord is our strength." (**Nehemiah 8:10**). The work of the ministry should be done with Joy. We need to serve the Lord with gladness. (**Psalms 100**)

Joy is mentioned 484 times in the Bible. **Dr. Jerry Savelle says:** "Joy is the thrust behind your faith. Joy will get your faith airborne! It gives wings to your faith!"

Developing the Fruit of Joy
You must develop a "knowing" to your joy. **James 1:2-3**. **Hebrews 12:2** - Knowing came from the Joy that was set before Him. Joy has the unique ability to focus on the final outcome of a situation and live in the celebration of triumph before it ever manifests. **Dr. Jerry Savelle says:** "When you find believers who are joyful whatever the circumstances may be, then you have found some winners. You can't beat a believer who is joyful."

Give voice to Joy (**Jeremiah 33:11**). Joy has a voice. Joy must express itself. Faith rejoices and praises. **I Chronicles 15:16**.

Times we are to release the force of Joy. (**Psalms 16:11**)
        1. Famine and lack (**Hebrews 3:17-18**)
        2. Persecution - (**Matt.5:12 Luke 6:23**)
        3. In Prison - (**Acts 16:23-25**)
        4. Loss of property or goods - (**Hebrews 10:34**)
        5. Fiery trials - (**1 Peter 4:12-13**)

You must guard and protect your joy. (**John 15:11**). **Negative bad news** can rob you of your joy – so always combat the world's news with God's Good News for that situation.

How Joy operates in obedience

Obedience will help release the force of joy on the inside of you. Serve the Lord with Joyfulness - **Deuteronomy 28:47-48**. We will operate in joy when we are walking in obedience.

The Fruit of Peace and its function

Peace is to bind together that which has been separated, the state of undisturbed, untroubled well-being, denoting the end of strife and the state of security.

The Biblical definition is found in Philippians 4:7 Amp. The tranquil state of a soul assured of its salvation through Jesus Christ, so fearing nothing from God and being content with it's earthly lot of whatever sort that is. It transcends all understanding and garrisons and mounts guard over hearts and minds in Christ Jesus.

Peace has been conferred on us by Jesus. (**John 14:27 John 16:33**). **Gloria Copeland says:** "True peace comes not from the absence of trouble, but from the presence of God, and will be deep and passing all understanding in the exact measure in which we live in and partake of the Love of God."

The function of Peace.
1. It acts as an umpire in our heart. (**Col. 3:15**). Peace acts as an umpire continually in our hearts deciding and settling with all finality, all questions that arise in our minds.
2. The Fruit of Peace will keep the believer safe within the boundaries of the Will of God. (**1 Corin. 14:33**)
3. God is the author of Peace, He is not the author of confusion.
4. Peace will permeate our relationships when we pursue after it. (**1 Peter 3:11**)

Developing the Fruit of Peace - Pursue it.

Things that will produce peace in our lives.
1. Resisting the spirit of fear. (**John 14:27**)
2. Our divine connection with Jesus. We have Peace with God through our Lord Jesus Christ. (**Romans 5:1**)

3. Being spiritually minded. (**Romans 8:6**)
4. Being controlled by the rule and authority of God.
   (**Romans 14:17**)
5. Thinking on things that are of God. (**Philippians 4:7-9**)
6. Allowing the Peace of God to rule in our hearts.
   (**Colossians 3:15**)
7. Obeying God's Word. (**Isaiah 48:18 Psalms 119:165**)
8. Prayer and Thanksgiving (**Philippians 4:6-7**)

The Fruit of Patience (Longsuffering)
Patience is a quality of self-restraint in the face of provocation which doesn't hastily retaliate or promptly punish. Patience is the quality that does not surrender to circumstances or succumb under trial.

Long suffering = patience with a purpose. Those that hear the Word with a good heart and keep the Word will bring forth the Fruit of Patience. (**Luke 8:15**)

Developing the Fruit of Patience
The testing of your faith will put patience to work. (**James 1:4**). Prayer will produce Patience. (**Colossians 1:9-11**). Staying connected to the Vine - Jesus (**John 15**)

Patience is vital to receiving
Patience will cause you to bare fruit. (**Luke 8:15**). Patience is the power of perseverance. (**2 Thessalonians 1:4**). **Gloria Copeland says:** "Patience is the force that keeps you from fainting under pressure". Faith and Patience work together, they are called the Power twins. (**Hebrews 6:11-15**).

The Fruit of Gentleness
Gentleness **is power under perfect control. I** quote from **Donald Gee - "**it takes part of the rugged strength of manhood and part of the controlled tenderness of womanhood to make the very finest gentleness. It is kindness in the very best way and fullest sense of the Word,"

Gentleness must never be confused with weakness. God is All powerful and Strong but He is also gentle. (**Isaiah 40:10-12**)

The need for the Fruit of Gentleness.
Gentleness is essentially in dealing with the souls of men. Must be gentle to all men. (**2 Timothy 2:24**). Gentleness is an essential requirement for a minister of the Gospel. A minister should not drive the sheep, but gently lead them. Practical areas where gentleness should be employed:

        1. Gentleness with our words (**Proverbs 15:1,4**)
        2. Church discipline (**Galatians 6:1 Amp**)
        3. Relationships (Marital) (**Colossians 3:19**)

Gentleness equips the Minister of God with skillfulness and sensitivity. The servant of the Lord must not strive, but must be gentle unto all men. (**2 Timothy 2:24**)

The Fruit of Goodness
Definition of Goodness - That quality in a man who rules and aims at what is good, namely; the quality of moral worth. The Greek defines "good men" as a promoter of virtue. Our lifestyle will preach louder than anything we can say. Qualifications for an elder. (**Titus 1:8**).

Passive Goodness.
The salt of the Earth.Goodness can be compared to the universal quality of salt. (**Matthew 5:13-16**).

Mark 9:50 - Salt is Good. Salt pulls the flavor out of food.We need to have people drawn to us.The Fruit of Goodness preserves the world from the corrupting power of sin. (**1 Corin. 15:33**)

Active Goodness.
It is an active manifestation of the Fruit of Goodness in the form of good works. Here are some scriptures on "Good works"

        1.   "Created in Christ Jesus unto good works." **Eph. 2:10**
        2.   "A peculiar people zealous of good works." **Titus 2:14**

3. "Let your light shine before men, that they may see your good works." **Matt. 5:16**
4. "That they which have believed in God might be careful to maintain good works." **Titus 3:8**
5. Paul proved his faith by good works. **James 2:17-18**

The Fruit of Meekness
Definition of meekness - "**Controlled Strength**" the state of being, which is to totally dependent on God. Jesus described Himself as meek and lowly of heart. (**Matthew 11:29**). The statement that Jesus made wasn't a statement of weakness. Meekness is not weakness. I quote from **Greg Zoschak's book "A Call for Character" (published by Tate Publishing) -** "Great meekness brings great power."

Meekness is a condition of the spirit; the heart. Meekness and gentleness are similar in many respects, but in this they are different. Meekness is inward but gentleness is outward (towards men.)

Meekness towards God.
Meekness points to a submissiveness of Spirit. Meekness is a condition of the spirit. (**Psalms 32:8**). Meekness always maintains a teachable spirit. (**James 1:21**)

Promises for the Meek.
"The meek shall eat and be satisfied." (**Psalms 22:26**). "The meek shall inherit the earth. (**Psalms 37:11 Matthew 5:5**). Meekness shall increase your joy. (**Isaiah 29:19**)

The Fruit of Faithfulness
Definition of faithfulness - To be trusted, reliable and loyal. When you are in ministry faithfulness is vital. Faithful men shall abound with blessings. (**Proverbs 28:20**)

Faithful originates with God.
He is a covenant keeping God. (**Deuteronomy 7:9 1 Thessalonians 5:24**)

God needs people in the Earth that have the same nature that He Himself has - **Faithfulness!**

Biblical examples of Faithfulness

Moses was faithful in all of God's house. (**Hebrews 3:5**). Daniel was faithful before men. (**Daniel 6:4**). Faithful in serving another. (**Proverbs 27:18**)

1. Joshua was faithful in serving Moses.
2. Elisha was faithful in serving Elijah.
3. Joseph was faithful in serving Potiphar.

Faithful men and woman are people who are faithful over what they already have. Parable of the talents. (**Matthew 25:15-23**). Faithful men are considered to be thoughtful and wise. (**Matthew 24:45). A faith man will rule**. One of the keys to true promotion is faithfulness. People with the Fruit of Faithfulness are willing to be faithful over little things. (**Matt 25:21).**

Faithfulness in ministry

Four areas that a minister is to be found faithful.

1. Faithful in preaching the Word of God. (**1 Timothy 4:2**)
2. Faithful in the matters of morality. (**Genesis 39:8-10**)
3. Faithful in keeping your word. (**Matthew 5:37**)
4. Faithful in business matters. (**2 Corin. 8:21**)

Faithfulness equips the believer. In stewardship over God's goods. With Joy of pleasing the Father. In believing that God is a covenant keeping God.

The Fruit of Self-Control (Temperance)

Definition of self control (temperance): Self restraint; inward strength. The Greek word rendered temperance in **Galatians 5:23** means self-control.

How Temperance will help you run and win. (1 Corin. 9:24-27 Moffat translation)

How to win and be successful in life
Man that competes for the prize is temperate in all things. (**1 Corin. 9:25-27**). The first step in running to win would be to become self-controlled and disciplined in all things. We must have self control and disciplined in our physical appetite, thought life, mouth and words, time with the Lord and in our finances. The Fruit of Temperance will keep you from being disqualified or castaway. (**1 Corin. 9:27**).

Chapter 11
A New Work

The Results of Maintaining a Lukewarm Spirit Where Service Is Concerned

Every Believer has been called to be a servant; however, many are not interested in serving. Your indifference to service results in procrastination and unfaithfulness. Considering all that God has done in your life, what are you doing for Him? How are you serving God and His kingdom? By serving God, you demonstrate your gratitude for all that He has done for you.

A lukewarm Christian has no zeal when it comes to serving God (Revelation 3:14-22).

God's goodness should propel you to serve Him (Nehemiah 9:35, *AMP*). It is right to be a servant of God. It is a sin to know what's right and not do it (James 4:17).

Things will cause you to procrastinate:

Worldly entanglement (i.e., your career and schedule).

Don't be slack in doing what God tells you to do. Lot was slack, and it almost cost him and his family their lives; however the mercy of God saved them (Genesis 19:15-16). When God—who knows everything—tells you to do something, obey Him immediately.

Family cares.

If you are going to follow Jesus, you must make *Him* your first priority (Matthew 8:20-22). Don't allow the cares of your family to distract you and prevent you from serving God (Luke 9:60-61). Your family will not suffer when God is at the top of your list of priorities. When you become successful in serving God, you will be successful in serving others. You must possess the heartbeat of servanthood, which is your desire to serve God. The best way to serve God is to serve His people.

Unbelief (Acts 17:32, *AMP*).
>When you are slow to believe, the spirit of procrastination is certain to show up in your life.

Personal convenience (Acts 24:25, *AMP*).
>Don't look for a convenient time to serve God.

You must be faithful to that which belongs to another (Luke 16:11-12).
>Serving someone who is anointed to do what you want to do will prepare you to be successful when you step out on your own. Elisha served Elijah, and as a result, he received a double portion of Elijah's anointing.

Overcoming the Spiritual Warning of Laodicea
Characteristics of new Christians include being on fire for God and having an unquenchable zeal for the things of the Lord. Young Christians are eager to learn and to be involved in everything their church has to offer. Unfortunately, over time, the fire and zeal begin to fade and are replaced with complacency, lukewarm feelings and indifference. It is time to rekindle the fire and continue gaining knowledge of God, as well as being busy in the things of God.

Rekindle your fire for God.
After becoming born again, joining a church and growing in the things of God, many people become complacent. *Complacent* means, "self-satisfied and unconcerned." It is a state of being happy with where you are and not desiring to move forward. The children of Israel became complacent in the wilderness. They were content to stay in the land of "just enough" instead of moving to the land of "more than enough."

People who do not want to be involved in church activities, who do not volunteer or who cut back on their church attendance use many excuses for not attending or being involved in church.

It's raining; I'm tired; I'm too busy, etc. The list can be endless. God will never become complacent toward us or our prayers. Take a moment to examine your life and ask: Where is my zeal? Where is my fire? What happened to my passion? Be careful not to neglect spending time at church with other Believers (Hebrews 10:25, *AMP*).

By coming together, people are able to encourage one another. People sometimes find it hard to stir themselves up and get excited about God after they have gained extensive knowledge about Him. It's up to the pastor to remind the congregation of what they know and for the people to remember what God has done for them (2 Peter 1:12-13).

Lukewarm is a better description of people's attitudes than complacency. It is described as not being zealous, which is being passionate, eager, enthusiastic, earnest, fervent and heartfelt. Newly born-again Christians are usually zealous.

Revelation 3:14-20 (*AMP*) is the only place in the Bible where the term *lukewarm* is used. God wanted the church of Laodicea to be either hot or cold instead of lukewarm. A lukewarm person causes God to vomit.

Some people who obtain wealth become lukewarm because they feel they have received everything that they need from God and don't need anything else from Him. These people do not realize that they have lost their zeal. Jesus said they are wretched, miserable, poor, blind and naked (v. 17, KJV). Jesus wants us to be truly wealthy, which we can only receive through Him by being "enthusiastic, earnest and burning with zeal" (v. 19, *AMP*).

The key to overcoming being lukewarm is to repent and have a change of attitude.
As a person continues to grow in the knowledge of God and His Word, the individual should continue to express passion, enthusiasm and zeal for the Lord (Romans 10:2).

Recognize key areas where indifference has entered your life.

Indifference is "being neutral; not interested; not leaning to one side or the other; a sense of apathy; impartial; unconcerned; to care less; middling; tolerable; absence of feeling; mediocrity."

The two areas where indifference invades one's life are: spiritually and in service. Check your spirit to determine if the spirit of indifference has invaded you spiritually. Are you at ease while others work for the kingdom (Psalm 123:4, *AMP*)?

The church is not supposed to be serving you; you are supposed to be serving the church. Don't allow ease to put you in neutral; you can't obtain God's promises in neutral. God commands you to rise up out of your position of ease (Isaiah 32:9).

An indifferent spirit causes you to sit safely and securely and keeps you from moving out of your comfort zone (Isaiah 47:8, *AMP*). People who feel condemned often stay away from the church (Isaiah 64:7). Don't allow the ease of staying at home keep you from fellowshipping with others.

On the other hand, don't shoot the wounded when they miss the mark. God warns those who are at ease in the church: You will inevitably face captivity (Amos 6:1, 7). Jesus warns that those who make light of His invitation to come to Him and decide to go their own way will not receive the blessings that He has prepared for them (Matthew 22:5).

It is important to have the love of God in your life and not to be indifferent, because the Bible warns that the love of many will grow cold, which will cause lawlessness inside and outside of the church (Matthew 24:12, *AMP*).

Indifference in service will lead to procrastination. The cares of family and worldly things will take precedence over the church's needs. Will you allow others to get involved in meeting the church's needs while you sit back and watch (Numbers 32:6)?

Where is your service? Ask yourself: How long will I be slack, or slow-moving, in regards to being in service to the church (Joshua 18:3)?

Printed in Great Britain
by Amazon

45983274R00047